YOU KNOW YOU'RE A TEXAN IF...

By Mike Nichols

Cartoons by J.D. Crowe

Book Design by Pinkney Media Group

A portion of the proceeds benefits
The North Fort Worth Historical Society
NFWHS STOCKYARDS MUSEUM

Great Texas Line Press

Bulk sales of books from Great Texas Line Press are available at special discounts for fund raising, promotions and premiums.

Great Texas Line Press
P.O. Box 11105
Fort Worth, Texas 76110

1-800-73TEXAS / Fax 817-926-0420

greattexas@hotmail.com
www.greattexasline.com

Great Texas Line Press strives to be a socially conscious publishing house. A portion of proceeds from several books is donated to worthy causes around the state, including Habitat for Humanity of Fort Worth, North Fort Worth Historical Society, Texas Dance Hall Inc. of Austin, and Big Bend Educational Foundation of Terlingua. Every effort is made to produce our books in Texas by family-run printing companies and to engage Texas writers, photographers, designers, illustrators and editors forced out of daily journalism by the newspaper industry crisis.

A Lone Star State of Mind
You know you're a Texan if:

You can distinguish a steer

from a bull just by the

wistful expression on the former's face.

3

You have cleaned one or more ears

with a **car key**.

You have cleaned one or more ears

with a **church key**.

You met your bride-to-be at a **gun show**.

You have placed wagers to win, place and show on a game of **cow patty bingo**.

You have programmed the phone number of your **taxidermist** on speed dial.

You have paid an east Dallas homeowner to let you **park your car** in his front yard during the **State Fair**.

You Know You're A Texan If:
You know what cow-tipping is and
you've never gone snipe hunting.

You remember exactly where you were

when you heard that **Troy Aikman** and

Lorrie Morgan had split.

You have played "connect the dots"

with your **fire ant stings**.

Your **all-Texan** version of **Mount Rushmore**

would feature the chiseled visages of Willie

Nelson, Nolan Ryan, Tom Landry

and Old Yeller.

You would leave a **dogfight** to attend a **cock-fight**, leave a cockfight to attend a **knife fight**, and leave a knife fight to watch two co-eds wrestle in **Jell-O**.

You think that Joyce Kilmer wrote his poem

with the **mesquite tree** in mind.

As a Boy Scout you earned a

Kickin' Ass merit badge.

You have been a finalist in the annual

Darwin Awards twice.

You think that **Greater Tuna** is a documentary

and that the guests on the **Jerry Springer**

show are normal.

A Loaf of Bread, A Jug of Wine, and Perhaps an Altoid
You know you're a Texan if:

On one or more occasions you have hired

Dairy Queen to cater a wedding.

You think that one of the four

major food groups is **Skoal**.

You have sold blood to get

money to **buy barbecue**.

You once held up a liquor store to

get money to **buy beer**.

You have insured the last surviving copy of

your mother's recipe for **Frito pie** with

Lloyd's of Lubbock.

You Know You're A Texan If:

You know that possums will eat anything

You know that the term **"chili con carne"** is redundant and that chili with **beans** is **an affront to nature**.

You have always assumed that **chicken- fried steak** and **Dr Pepper** were served at the Last Supper.

You reckon that if the gods of ancient Greece and Rome were around today, they'd put **Ranch dressing** on their **ambrosia**.

You feel that if **God** had intended for us

not to eat jalapenos, He would

have given us **good sense**.

Fashions
You know you're a Texan if:

Your husband's **belt buckle** is so big and round that it affects local tides.

Your wife's **hairdo** is so big and round that it has smaller hairdos orbiting around it.

As a woman, if your home were on fire, the first thing you'd rush in to rescue is your **beauty cream**.

As a man, if your home were on fire,

the first thing you'd rush in to rescue

is your wife's **beauty cream**.

You don't look twice at men who

wear **bib overalls**.

You feel that if God had intended for us **not to**

get tattoos . . . see jalapenos entry.

PASSIONS
You know you're a Texan if:

In your wallet you carry a snapshot of

your **bass boat**.

Around your house, when you

refer to "**Shoog**," you might be

referring to your **wife, your dog**,

or **your shotgun.**

The store where you buy bait also sells

fireworks, wigs, and Bibles.

19

You Know You're A Texan If:

You have a dog and a
brother-in-law named Bud.

 You know that a **goldfish** is just a carp who has a good PR agent and that a **dove** is just a pigeon who has been to finishing school.

On the Internet your name comes up if someone Googles **"freak hunting accident."**

On New Year's Day you eat **black-eyed peas**; on the day after deer season opens you eat **venison**; and all too often in recent years on the day after the Red River Shootout

you eat **crow**.

You have put off until halftime

going to the **bathroom**.

You have put off until halftime

going to the **emergency room**.

You have put off until halftime

going to the **delivery room**.

You have gotten

into a fistfight during a **game of poker**.

You have gotten into a fistfight during

a **game of bridge**.

To you, **fighting words include state income

tax**, gun control, near beer, tofu and Alaska.

You begged your wife to let you **name your

first child "NASCAR."** Clenching her teeth, she

replied: "Sure thing, Hon. But only if you'll let me

name our second child after its **real father**."

23

You Know You're A Texan If:
You think the first day of deer hunting season
is a national holiday.

HAND CLAPPIN' 'N' TOE TAPPIN'
You know you're a Texan if:

You have posted a **Youtube** video clip of your-

self lip-synching the Dixie Chicks'

"White Trash Wedding."

After you die, the first two questions you are going to ask Saint Peter are:

1. Which cloud is the Lone Star State Celestial Band (Janis Joplin, Stevie Ray Vaughan, Roy Orbison, Buddy Holly, Ernest Tubb and Waylon Jennings) jamming on? and

2. Is there a cover?

Your **first child** was conceived

after a **ZZ Top** concert.

Your first child's first child was conceived

after a **ZZ Top** concert.

27

You Know You're A Texan If:
You fall in love with the first person you see
when you hear Bob Wills's **"Faded Love."**

28

HIS'N AND HER'N
You know you're a Texan if:

As a woman you can get past a five-strand

barbed-wire fence with nary a

scratch to hide or hose.

As a man you can string five strands of barbed wire on fence posts so tautly that you could play **"Dueling Banjos"** on them.

As a man you have cried while trading in a faithful **pickup truck**, giving away a litter of **hounds**, and watching the **Texas Rangers** make a pitching change.

As a woman, in your **divorce settlement** you

demanded custody of the children but granted

your husband custody of the twins –

his two **Evinrudes**.

As a man, **you don't remember** your wed-

ding anniversary or your wife's birthday, but

you remember the Alamo, **two-dollar**

gasoline, one-dollar cigarettes,

and the opening day lineup

of the 1962 Houston Astros.

As a woman **you remember** your wedding anniversary, your husband's birthday, what he was wearing the night you met him, the song you two were dancing to when he first kissed you, and what his **blood alcohol level** was the night he proposed.

FURRINERS
You know you're a Texan if:

You think of Louisiana as "back east."

You think of Oklahomans as "northerners."

You think of **New Mexicans** as "them folks

way the hell over thataway."

You think of **Mexico as a suburb of Laredo**.

When you die you want your ashes to be

scattered over a **Yankee's clam chowder**.

Tejas Means "All Who Are Friends"

You know you're a Texan if:

When driving **you lift one hand slightly off the steering wheel** as a greeting when **passing a total stranger**.

You precede a tacky remark about someone with "**Bless his/her heart.**"

You **start conversations with strangers** while standing in line at the supermarket or bank.

You address people as "**Ma'am**" and "**Sir**" even if they are **younger** than you.

You feel that it is impolite to hang up on phone solicitors – even recorded messages.

You once **talked on the phone for twenty minutes to a wrong number**. You still get Christmas cards from her.

GOING PLACES IN WIDE, OPEN SPACES

You know you're a Texan if:

You have **driven ten miles**

to visit a "**neighbor**."

You measure distance in tanks of gasoline.

You know that mathematically the **shortest**

distance between two points is closed

due to **road construction.**

You have made a **pilgrimage** to Stanley

Marsh III's **Cadillac Ranch**.

You have a bumper sticker that reads

"My other car is a truck."

You have a bumper sticker that reads

"My other car is a tractor."

You have a bumper sticker that reads

"My other car is a horse."

You have been sure in **Uncertain**,

sad in Happy, and dissonant in **Harmony**.

You have had little pep in Energy but had

oodles in **Noodle**, especially

after a cup in **Coffee City**.

You have been eighter from Decatur, turned

east in West, **bounced a check in Cash**, seen

todo in Nada, been at your worst in Best,

gone ape in Tarzan, caused a stink in Fink,

been on the **blink in Wink**,

and had a **conniption fit in Grit**.

41

You have whistled in Dixie, changed your mind in Choice, worn a **pompadour in Flat Top**, and met your **destiny in Fate**.

When your **twenty-year-old Chevy half-ton** finally dies, you plan to have the engine **cryogenically preserved** in the hope that someday medical science will discover a cure for vapor lock.

You have adapted an old cowboy philosophy to driving fast in Texas:

When you're out there on the trail, ridin' ahead of that herd of cattle, Pard, it's a good idea to look behind you every now and then to be sure none of 'em has a radar gun.

You know that **more flags have flown over this state than over this nation**.

You know that when you are in Newton County you are **closer to the Atlantic Ocean than to El Paso** and that when you are in El Paso you are closer to the Pacific Ocean than to Newton County.

And when you are in Brownsville, a **beer run to Guatemala would be shorter** than one to Dalhart.

You know that the **King Ranch**, at 825,000 acres, **is larger than Rhode Island**.

You know that when four vehicles arrive at a four-way stop at the same time in Dumas, **the pickup with the biggest stock trailer** has the right-of-way.

You know that when four vehicles arrive at a four-way stop at the same time in Dallas, the SUV with **the biggest fold-down DVD monitor** has the right-of-way.

THE CHILL IN CHILDRESS, THE PERSPIRATION IN COLLEGE STATION

You know you're a Texan if:

You have **worn shorts and later an overcoat**,

have drunk iced tea and later hot chocolate,

have suffered sunburn and later frostbite

all on the same day.

You Know You're A Texan If:
You grasp Texas summer chemistry:
Water becomes a gas, creek beds
become a solid and asphalt becomes a liquid.

You have documented storms by **putting hailstones in your freezer**. It would hold only two.

Your children's school cancels classes when there is a twenty percent **chance of scattered snow flurries**.

49

To you, **white Christmas is just a song title**.

In summer you have received second-degree

burns from the **upholstery of your car**.

In August you choose **parking spaces**

based on shade, not distance.

You consider ninety degrees to be mild and

sixty degrees to be "a bit nippish."

You don't **consider summer to have officially**

begun until you hear the **first locust buzz.**

51

You begin **saving in April to pay** your **electric bill** in August.

You can steer a horse over a **barrel racing course**, a Jet Ski over a choppy lake, and an ATV over rocks and ruts but **can't steer a car over the patchiest ice**.

Each tornado season you are interviewed by local TV news reporters because "**I heard what sounded like a freight train**, see, and the next thing **I knew my single-wide was upside-down at the far end of Aluminum Acres**, and there was my toilet hanging from the floor which was now the ceiling like one of **them stalagmites**.

Or stalactites. I disremember which. A fat

lot of good that toilet is going to do me up

there! I mean I'm as tall in the saddle as the

next guy, if you catch my drift, but . . . say,

reckon you could get me a date

with the **weather girl?**"

TALK THE TALK, WALK THE MOSEY

You know you're a Texan if:

You use the terms **pert near**, smack dab, **yea big**, and scootch as **units of measurement**.

You know that yonder is a measure of distance, directly **is a measure of time**.

You use the verbs **tump**, **reckon**, **waller**, **fixin' to**, a-wolfin', and scootch ("Scootch over this- away just a scootch, Darlin'.").

You can use the terms **cattywampus** and **honkerjawed** (adjectives describing a poor fit) in a sentence without giggling.

You know that **prairie oysters are not mollusks**, that meadow muffins have never been anywhere near an oven, that road apples don't fall from a tree, and that there was precious little poultry at the Chicken Ranch.

You feel that **anyone who pronounces the "g"** in the suffixing or says "San Antonio" instead of "San Antone" is **putting on airs**.

You have bet your **boots**, your **britches**, and your **bottom dollar**.

You know that **y'all is singular**,

all y'all is plural.

You know that **there is no r in "Foat Wuth,"**

no wax in "Waxahachie," and **no mex in**

"Mexia," but there is **a witch in "Wichita**

Falls" and a way down in "Joshua."

When circumstances warrant,

you know how to **mosey, traipse, sashay,**

skedaddle and hightail it.

WE OF A CERTAIN AGE REMEMBER

You know you're a Texan if:

You remember when Texans **couldn't shop on a Sunday**, bank at a branch, buy a lottery ticket or liquor by the drink, **bet on a horse**, or turn right on red after stop. Now you can indulge in all of those once-forbidden activities. Go ahead. Pack a picnic lunch.

Make a day of it.

You Know You're A Texan If:
You know which tree leaves make
good toilet paper.

You have rubbed a **horny toad's belly** to make it go to sleep, caught lightning bugs in a jar, rescued a box turtle from the middle of a highway, and voted the Democratic ticket.

You call a refrigerator an "ice box," Interstate 30 in Fort Worth-Dallas "the Turnpike," margarine "oleo," the accelerator pedal the "foot-feed," and middle school "junior high."

Your introduction to poetry was

Burma-Shave signs.

Your mother threatened to

"**wash your mouth** out with **Bab-o**."

Your father threatened to "**tan your hide**."

One or more parents warned you that **"if you don't leave that** [insert animal of choice] alone, you'll **pull back a nub**."

You were baptized in a river, were bathed in a galvanized tub, were taught to swim in a stock tank, caught tadpoles in a bar ditch, then survived three droughts and now read a full rain gauge as if it were a beatitude.

You have addressed a woman as **"little heifer."** You still have the scars.

GAWD'S COUNTRY
You know you're a Texan if:

You are a **Baptist born and bred**, never saw a Methodist until you were twelve years old, and have heard that a **closet Unitarian** lives down the street but personally don't believe it.

Your church sanctuary's stained-glass depiction

of **Noah's ark includes a pair of armadillos**.

You have taken a covered dish of

potato salad to a bereaved household.

You have worn **jeans to a funeral**.

No one noticed.

You know that it really is a sin to

kill a mockingbird.

You believe that on the sixth day **the Lord made the Hill Country** and that on **the seventh day he rested by tubing down the Guadalupe**.

Classics We Couldn't Resist

(If anyone claims authorship, let us know
and we'll give credit in the next edition)

You know you're a Texan if:

You know there are **5,000 types of snakes**,

and 4,998 of them are native to Texas.

You Know You're A Texan If:

You know armadillos sleep in the middle
of the road with their feet in the air.

You know that **onced and twiced**

are legitimate words.

You know that the phrase, "**He finished first in**

his class," means "**he dropped out first**."

71

You know that when you live in the country, you don't have to buy a dog. **City people drop them off** at your gate in the middle of the night.

You think the first day of **deer season is a national holiday**.

You **consulted a football schedule** when planning your wedding date.

You know that a seat belt makes an **effective branding iron**.

72

You Know You're A Texan If:
You know when a buzzard sits on the fence and
stares at you, it's time to go to the doctor.

You Know You're A Texan If:

You know nothing will kill a mesquite tree.

You can **distinguish a rock** from
an armadillo at **three hundred yards**.

You know the difference among **one-alarm,
two-alarm, and three-alarm chili**.

You **choose a bottle of salsa** as carefully as
another person might choose a bottle of wine.
(Source: austin.about.com)

Never ask a man if he's from Texas.
If he is, he'll tell you on his own. If he ain't,
no need to embarrass him.

You Know You're A Texan If:

You know that "Je'eet?" is a
contraction of "Did you eat?"

You can always **tell a Texan**,

but you **can't tell him much**.

[You might be a real Texan if]

If your family business requires a lookout.
(Source: onceuponasmile.blogspot.com)

You know that a **traffic jam** involves two drivers staring each other down at a **four-way stop**, each determined to be the more polite and let the other go first.
(Source: weirytraveler.blogspot.com)

77

You consider a **televised football game fol-lowed by a wrestling match** to be a double feature.

(Source phatmass.com)

You think the concluding words of the **"Star-Spangled Banner"** are **"Gentlemen, start your engines."**

You've been **married three times** and still have the same in-laws.

And you just might could be a **pure-dee, sure-'nuff, rootin'-tootin'** Texan if you know when it's time to say, **"That's all she wrote."**

78

Y'ALL COME BACK REAL SOON NOW, Y'HEAR?